CHRONICLES

CHRONICLES

Written by
STEVE BYNGHALL

CONTENTS

HELLO FROM THE HELPERS
(AND AN EVIL PORTAL MASTER)

Are you ready for the adventure of a lifetime? If the answer is yes, then join us! Prepare to visit the most incredible islands and remarkable realms. Meet bizarre beings and discover their magical abilities. Battle against thoroughly evil enemies and help defend Skylands!

These friendly residents of Skylands aren't Skylanders, but they are dedicated to protecting their home from evil. Never fear, as these brave helpers will always be by your side while you explore their amazing world.

There are many places to see and even more people to meet, so enjoy your trip, and welcome to Skylands!

FLYNN

> WELL, HEY THERE, ADVENTURER. THE NAME'S FLYNN, AND FLYING IS MY GAME. IF YOU ARE NEW TO SKYLANDS, THEN YOU'LL NEED MY HELP GETTING TO KNOW THESE CRAZY ISLANDS. I'M ALWAYS HAPPY TO GIVE A FRIEND A RIDE, AND IF YOU'RE HELPING THE SKYLANDERS, THAT MAKES YOU A FRIEND. BOOM!

HUGO

HELLO!
VERY PLEASED TO MEET YOU!
I'VE ASSISTED MASTER EON FOR MANY YEARS,
SO I KNOW ALL ABOUT GOINGS-ON IN SKYLANDS.
I ALSO LOVE HISTORY, SO IF YOU EVER NEED
TO KNOW ABOUT SKYLANDS' PAST,
COME AND FIND ME.

CALI

LISTEN UP.
SKYLANDS IS A GREAT PLACE, BUT IT CAN BE
DANGEROUS. YOU'LL NEED TO GET THE LOW-DOWN
ON ALL THE TROUBLEMAKERS AROUND HERE, AS WELL
AS LEARNING FROM OUR BRAVE SKYLANDERS.
KEEP YOUR EYES AND EARS OUT, SO YOU
ARE READY FOR ANYTHING.

MWAHAHA!
I AM KAOS, GREATEST OF ALL THE
PORTAL MASTERS AND SOON-TO-BE RULER OF
SKYLANDS. AT LEAST, I WOULD BE IF THOSE PESKY
SKYLOSERS DIDN'T KEEP INTERRUPTING ALL OF MY
GENIUS PLANS. BOW DOWN TO ME, FOOLS,
OR FACE THE CONSEQUENCES...

KAOS

PORTAL MASTER
TRAINING

Greetings, young Portal Master. I have been waiting for you. I am Eon.

Skylands is a magical world of wonder and adventure, protected by the greatest heroes ever known: the Skylanders.

It has long been my duty to watch over the Skylanders and lead them, but this task has now been given to you.

Portal Masters choose brave souls to become Skylanders and can control magical portals between realms.

We must all work together to keep the peace in Skylands.

Portal Masters are summoned in times of great need.

Something evil is stirring. Skylands is in danger.

A great quest awaits you, young Portal Master. I have sent my assistant Hugo to seek you out. We will speak again soon.

TOP TIPS FOR SUCCESS

Watch out for a small ugly chap going on about wanting to take over Skylands. That's Kaos! Don't underestimate him...

They may look to you for guidance, but the Skylanders are not the slaves of Portal Masters. Skylanders serve their Portal Masters willingly and should always be treated with respect.

When I was young, I was the servant boy of the great Portal Master, Nattybumpo. One day I accidently activated a portal and teleported him to the Dirt Seas. Never do this to me, young Portal Master.

No pressure, young Portal Master, but the future of Skylands rests entirely in your hands. So you had better keep calm.

WELCOME TO SKYLANDS

Skylands is an immense expanse of different and distant islands that float upon an endless sky. It is a magical world filled with wonder and mystery, where just about anything can happen. There are amazing places to explore and incredible creatures to meet. Wherever you are in Skylands, get set for adventure!

TERRAINS

Skylands has too many floating islands to count, and each of them has a unique terrain. There are glistening lagoons, mighty mountains, snowy wastelands, grassy pastures, and cloudy kingdoms.

PORTALS

Skylands is huge! In fact, nobody even knows where it begins or ends. The quickest way to travel around is through portals: magical doorways that connect one part of Skylands with another.

QUIRKY CHARACTERS

Weird and wonderful species live in Skylands. They can be strange, dangerous, silly, or fierce. From scary-looking skeletons to grass-munching sheep, all of life is here!

DARK AND LIGHT

A dangerous force called the Darkness is an ever-present threat to Skylands. It spreads evil and chaos. An ancient machine called the Core of Light holds the Darkness at bay.

PROTECTORS

An elite band of heroes known as the Skylanders keeps Skylands safe. They defend Skylands from the forces of Darkness and protect the Core of Light.

POWER OF THE ELEMENTS

There are eight known elements flowing all around Skylands. They are the essence of everything that exists in it. Each of the elements has strengths and weaknesses, but they are all equally important.

MAGIC

Many Skylanders consider Magic to be the most important element because it is what fuels the special powers of the other seven elements. Skylanders who belong to the Magic element are known for their powers of sorcery and tremendous trickery.

TECH

Skylanders with Tech as their element are no geeks! Some Tech Skylanders harness the power of machinery to build awesome weaponry and other ingenious contraptions. The power of Tech has been used in Skylands since ancient times.

EARTH

The element Earth is found all over Skylands, in everything from the dirtiest mud to the most precious mineral. Skylanders with the Earth element rock! They often use rocks and crystals to destroy the enemy.

UNDEAD

The shadowy Undead element may seem both ghostly and ghastly, but it isn't as sinister as it sounds. Undead Skylanders have many scare tactics, from bolts of spectral lightning to just being plain frightening, but their dark powers are usually used for good.

UNDEAD

MAGIC

TECH

EARTH

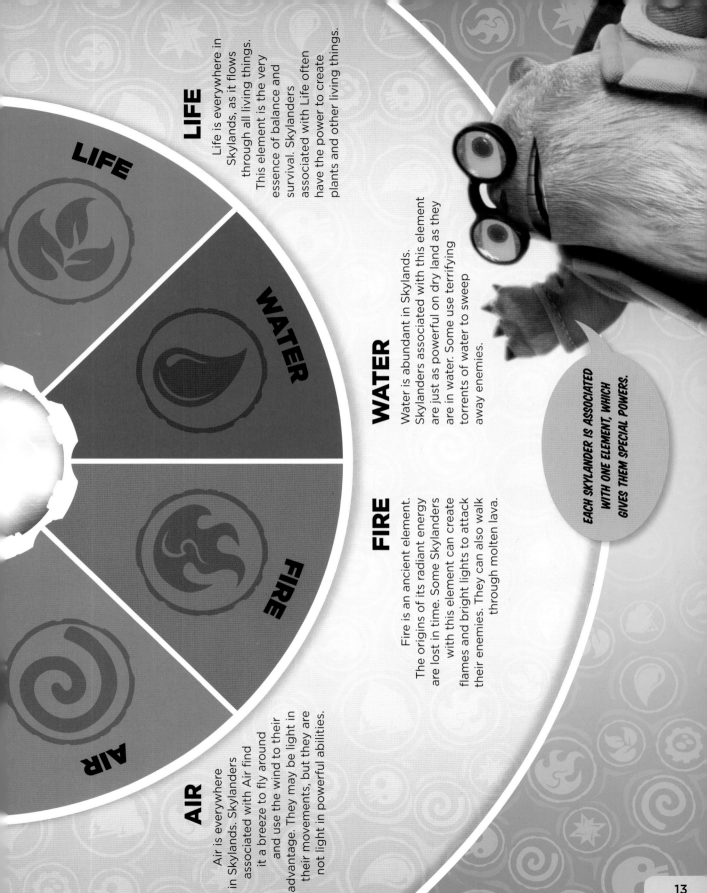

LIFE

Life is everywhere in Skylands, as it flows through all living things. This element is the very essence of balance and survival. Skylanders associated with Life often have the power to create plants and other living things.

WATER

Water is abundant in Skylands. Skylanders associated with this element are just as powerful on dry land as they are in water. Some use terrifying torrents of water to sweep away enemies.

FIRE

Fire is an ancient element. The origins of its radiant energy are lost in time. Some Skylanders with this element can create flames and bright lights to attack their enemies. They can also walk through molten lava.

AIR

Air is everywhere in Skylands. Skylanders associated with Air find it a breeze to fly around and use the wind to their advantage. They may be light in their movements, but they are not light in powerful abilities.

EACH SKYLANDER IS ASSOCIATED WITH ONE ELEMENT, WHICH GIVES THEM SPECIAL POWERS.

13

WHO ARE THE SKYLANDERS?

There are a few things that most people know about the Skylanders: They are clever, courageous, and committed to defending Skylands from evil forces. But what else is there to know about this hardy group of heroes? Where did they come from and what makes them as important as they are in Skylands?

THE FIRST SKYLANDERS WERE THE GIANTS

The Giants were the very first Skylanders. A long time ago, the Giants banded together to battle an ancient civilization called the Arkeyans, who ruled Skylands with an iron fist. Each of the Giants is aligned with one of the eight elements of Skylands, and they all have incredible levels of strength.

WASH BUCKLER

JET-VAC

COUNTDOWN

STEALTH ELF

THEY ARE DEFENDERS OF A HUB WORLD

It is important that the Skylanders protect Skylands because it is a world between worlds. From Skylands, it is possible to jump to any point in the universe through magical portals. If evil forces ever manage to take over Skylands, they could then travel to anywhere else in the universe—including Earth.

THEY ARE CHOSEN AND GUIDED BY A PORTAL MASTER LIKE EON

Portal Masters are the wise beings from all worlds and dimensions who choose and guide the Skylanders as they defend Skylands. Master Eon is the greatest of them all. He is training a new generation of Portal Masters.

GENERALLY, NO RULES APPLY

ERUPTOR

TERRAFIN

MAGNA CHARGE

There is no such thing as a typical Skylander! They can come from any corner of Skylands or be drawn from any species. Each individual hero has their own special skills and powers, too. It is this unique mix of different backgrounds and abilities that helps make the Skylanders so successful at defending Skylands.

RUINED REMAINS

THE LOST CITY

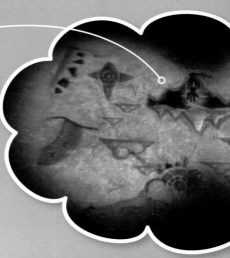

CORE OF LIGHT BASE

ROBOT ARMY

Kaos thinks reactivating an army of ancient Arkeyan robots will help in his quest for power. To recover these mighty machines, he first needs to find their lost city, Arkus. He won't get far with an upside-down map, though!

CORE OF LIGHT

For centuries, the Core of Light kept the Darkness at bay with its protective beam of light. That was, until Kaos caused it to explode, scattering the Skylanders to Earth. Now they are back, Kaos is determined to stop them rebuilding it and returning order to Skylands.

THREATS TO SKYLANDS

All is not well in Skylands. An evil Portal Master known as Kaos wishes to rule over it, and he is full of dastardly plots and cunning conspiracies to help him fulfill his dream. Some of his plans may sound far-fetched, but the risk to Skylands is serious. It is up to the noble Skylanders to defend their world against Kaos's dreams of destruction, evil forces, and dark magic. The Skylanders must always be on guard, for whenever Kaos is defeated, you can guarantee that he is dreaming up another equally evil plan!

IRON FIST
If he finds Arkus, Kaos hopes to discover the legendary Iron Fist of the Arkeyan Kings. Not only does it reawaken and control the robot army, it even has the power to turn Kaos into a huge Arkeyan robot!

THE IRON FIST

EVIL ERUPTION

Another of Kaos's dastardly plans is to pack the magical Mount Cloudbreak volcano with evilizing Petrified Darkness crystals. These purple gems have the power to make everyone as horrible as Kaos! If the volcano erupts, the whole of Skylands will be evilized.

EVIL IDEAS FORMING

Did you know?
Kaos's first plan to take over Skylands was to simply build statues of himself everywhere. He thought everyone would assume he was their ruler. They didn't.

THE MINIONS OF KAOS

GREEBLES

Did you know?

Kaos's most loyal helper is his butler, Glumshanks. When Kaos needed a date to the school prom, he even made Glumshanks go with him.

The little man with the huge ego might think he is awesome enough to carry out his evil ambition to take over Skylands on his own, but he's not. Take a peek inside Kaos's Frighter Fax to meet a selection of the vile minions that help him with his mean schemes... if you dare!

DROWS

My Drows are delightfully evil elves. Armored Lance Masters are just one of a variety of Drow. They never miss a target with their lethal lances. But if they do, I get very, VERY ANGRY. My mother's not keen on them—their lances are very big, and she's had a few near misses—but what does she know?

Fright factor: 10

Note to self: If all else fails, evilize a SKYLANDER!

K-BOTS

In case you hadn't realized, I'm a very big deal, so I have my own robot security force, called K-Bots, to keep irksome intruders out of my fortress. The most dreaded of these droids are the K-Bot Mineminers. One sniff of an interloper and the Mineminers release their homing rockets, then KABOOM! Goodbye, Skylanders!

Fright factor: 9

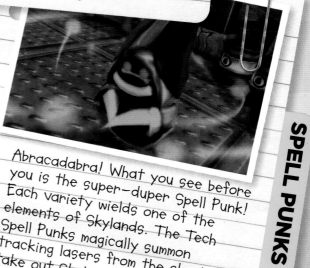

Ahh, here we have my Geargolems. Each type of these sinister robots has a dangerous skill. Take the Air Geargolems. They use an air jet current to suck in pesky Skylanders or anything else that gets in their way. They dislike sheep, which is no bad thing in my opinion—and my opinion is the only one that matters.

Fright factor: 5

th ha. This is one of my proudest creations. I bring to you... the Evilized Greeble! I tried using the regular Greebles, but they were rubbish so I evilized them! They slash their cutlasses with great gusto. Actually, sometimes too much gusto if I'm standing near them.

Fright factor: 8

Abracadabra! What you see before you is the super-duper Spell Punk! Each variety wields one of the elements of Skylands. The Tech Spell Punks magically summon tracking lasers from the sky to take out Skylanders. They are not as powerful as me, but who is?

Fright factor: 6

Yes, yes, so all of my Trolls might be one-trick monkeys but the little brutes get the job done, OK? These Troll Greasemonkeys slam their wrenches down on enemies with frightening force. My Trolls fear nothing. Well, apart from me of course.

Fright factor: 7

FEAR THEM! FEAR EVERY ONE OF MY MIGHTY MINIONS!

MASTER EON

Master Eon started life as a humble servant boy before he discovered his amazing abilities as a Portal Master. He recruited Skylanders to fight evil forces in Skylands and became the greatest and wisest Portal Master that ever was.

HUGO HIDES

As the years went by, Master Eon knew that, one day, evil forces would try to destroy the Core of Light. And he was right! (He is very, very wise.) When that day arrived, I dived into a manhole. From my hiding place, I was able to witness the epic battle for Skylands that unfolded.

THE DAY OF THE DARKNESS

Hugo's love for history is almost as huge as his hatred for sheep. The knowledgeable historian has chronicled the major events of Skylands and even witnessed some of them himself. No event in Skyland's history has had more impact than the day the forces of Darkness destroyed the Core of Light. Luckily, Hugo lived to tell the tale...

THIS HISTORIC DAY IS ETCHED IN MY MEMORY, JUST AS IF IT HAPPENED YESTERDAY.

ENTER KAOS

The evil Portal Master known as Kaos emerged as a giant head to take over Skylands. His huge head might look frightening, but in reality he is a tiny pipsqueak.

EXPLOSION

Kaos unleashed his ultimate weapon—a terrifying, four-headed dragon called the Hydra. The brave Skylanders battled hard against the beast. However, the Hydra caused the Core of Light to explode, scattering it to the far corners of Skylands.

DOWN TO EARTH

Using the power of Magic, Kaos banished the Skylanders all the way to planet Earth. Without the magic of Skylands around them, they shrank and became frozen, like toys. The only way they would get back to Skylands was if a Portal Master found them on Earth.

BRAVERY

SLOBBER TOOTH

POWERFUL TAIL

Being a Skylander means facing incredible danger every day. Courage is a necessity—there is no room for nerves or hesitation in this job. Slobber Tooth once took on Kaos and his minions single-handedly, and daredevil Trigger Happy is always taking crazy risks!

TRIGGER HAPPY

RECKLESS RIDE

WHAT ARE THE
QUALITIES OF A
SKYLANDER?

Master Eon picks only the best heroes to become Skylanders. One in a million has what it takes to join this elite force. Fighting ability is important, but it is not the only thing Eon is looking for. Any potential Skylander must also demonstrate they have the right attitude to protect Skylands.

HONOR

FIERY FISTS

BLIZZARD CHILL

Many Skylanders are motivated by a sense of honor and duty. They know right from wrong, and are determined to bring evil forces to justice. Tough guy Fryno was outraged to discover his biker buddies were crooks, so he taught them that crime does not pay. Blizzard Chill learned her sense of duty as a Royal Guard, and never forgets her loyalty to her Queen.

ICE JAVELIN

FRYNO

DETERMINATION

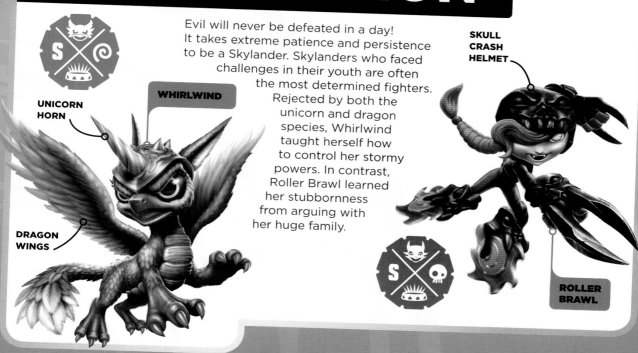

Evil will never be defeated in a day! It takes extreme patience and persistence to be a Skylander. Skylanders who faced challenges in their youth are often the most determined fighters. Rejected by both the unicorn and dragon species, Whirlwind taught herself how to control her stormy powers. In contrast, Roller Brawl learned her stubbornness from arguing with her huge family.

UNICORN HORN

WHIRLWIND

DRAGON WINGS

SKULL CRASH HELMET

ROLLER BRAWL

INTELLIGENCE

Kaos and his cronies are always carrying out cunning plans. Skylanders need to draw on all their intelligence and wisdom to outwit the enemy! Trap Shadow shows great ingenuity in setting his hidden traps, and Zoo Lou's shamanic wisdom helps him channel the power of nature.

MAGICAL STAFF

ZOO LOU

TRAP SHADOW

CAMOUFLAGE MARKINGS

ANIMAL MASCOT BELT

TRAP

REALMS OF SKYLANDS

Skylands is vast, with many islands and kingdoms to explore. No two places, or their inhabitants are ever the same. Unfortunately, wherever you choose to go, definite danger lies ahead. With Kaos and his minions around, it seems that every realm is packed with perils and threats.

CUTTHROAT CARNIVAL

Cutthroat Carnival is the most unfair fairground around. Here, you are likely to be taken for a ride, and not in a good way. That's because all the attractions are run by a group of pirates. It's more of a pirate hideout than a fun day out. The one-eyed bandits at the carnival love to engage visitors in a game of Skystones. But proceed with caution—pirates never play by the rules!

RUMBLETOWN

Rumbletown used to be a pleasant place until Brock, a Goliath Drow, strolled into town. Now it's overrun with Spell Punks, Root Runners, and various other nasties. You might meet Ermit the Hermit here. He isn't really a hermit—he is actually a people person, but he does have has a terrible fear of clouds.

ERMIT THE HERMIT

RAMPANT RUINS

The Rampant Ruins is full of grave dangers. The robots who are buried here were once powered by Petrified Darkness crystals, and now they are coming back to life! A Grave Monkey has stood guard over the graveyard for centuries, eating bananas and stamping on robots that rise from their graves.

GRAVE MONKEY

WINTER KEEP

Home to the friendly Frost Elves, the snowy wastelands of Winter Keep are a wondrous sight. This land fell under a curse that meant it was always midnight. These days, the curse is kept at bay by a magical horn known as the Illuminator, which was created by Air Skylander Whirlwind. The horn brings permanent daylight to Winter Keep, which can make it difficult to sleep at night.

THE ILLUMINATOR

WILIKIN VILLAGE

Welcome to Wilikin Village, a playful place where everyone's a friend! Except for the Chompies who also live here. The Wilikin Dolls were Kaos's childhood dolls. He brought them to life when he was a child—the lonely boy needed some friends to play with!

WILIKIN DOLL

WHO LIVES IN SKYLANDS?

It would take a long time to list all the creatures and beings that live in Skylands, and that's only the ones that are known about! Life is varied here and its inhabitants couldn't be more different from each other. Many have built up their own civilizations and cities all over the land. Some creatures, like Gillmen, are common sights, while others are much harder to find.

POWERFUL MALLETS TO WREAK REVENGE WITH

LONG BRANCHES USED TO BE HERE

STUMP SMASH
Skylander Stump Smash is a bit of a grump. He still bears a grudge against the Trolls, who chopped off his long branches.

ENT

Ent are tree-like forest-dwellers. They are usually peaceful by nature and have excellent memories. Many Ent, such as Arbo and Stump Smash, are also helpful and willing to lend a helping branch to Skylanders and Portal Masters in need.

ARBO
Friendly Arbo sprouted during Kaos's evil reign. He is always happy to share his knowledge with the Skylanders to help them save the day.

FROST ELVES

It's hard to miss the friendly Frost Elves, with their distinctive blue skin and pointy ears. Hailing from the mysterious Cloudbreak Islands, they are all incredibly proud, brave, and loyal.

AVRIL
Avril might be the youngest of twelve, but she's no pushover—which is why the Snow King made her Captain of the Frost Elf Guard.

SNOWBALL FUN
It wouldn't be wise to take on the Frost Elves in a snowball fight—they have had years of practice and always come out on top!

GURGLEFIN
When he's not offering his assistance to help save Skylands, Gurglefin can usually be found playing the game Skystones.

MOLEKIN

Molekin are small, short-sighted, mole-like creatures. As well as being highly intelligent, they are very helpful and polite. Molekin are also naturally good with their paws, and are known for being particularly skilled miners. They are useful allies for the Skylanders.

Did you know?
The Molekin used to use oil as a hair tonic. Unfortunately, it made their hair fall out! Now, the Molekin only use oil in machinery, as they are all completely bald.

DIGGS
Diligent worker Diggs might have extremely poor eyesight, but he is still a brilliant engineer. He's also an enthusiastic trainspotter.

GILLMEN

Gillmen inhabit the watery areas of Skylands. They have a reputation for being reliable and are valuable allies to have. Gillmen also have the worst singing voices in the whole of Skylands, but they think this dreadful racket sounds beautiful.

GILL GRUNT
Gutsy Skylander Gill Grunt is adventurous and a true warrior. He wields his harpoon gun with great skill.

MAGIC

Magic is the mightiest element of all. It is the force that binds all of Skylands together and the essence of all its creatures, from the Skylanders to the sheep. Magic's amazing powers can be used for good, but they can also be used for evil.

QUICKSILVER

Quicksilver is a mysterious ancient oil that provides the essence of all things magic in Skylands. It is a vital component of the Core of Light, but it was flung far away when the magical machine was destroyed. This strange and wonderful substance can now be found hidden deep inside an Arkeyan Vault.

MAGICAL MOB

These Magic Skylanders might look like a crazy crew, but be under no illusion—you don't want to mess with these guys! Magic Skylanders can conjure up tricks, spells, and assorted sorcery to battle their opponents.

SUPER GULP POP FIZZ

MEGA-RAM SPYRO

STAR STRIKE

DUNE BUG

HOOT LOOP

TRAP SHADOW

SPYRO

Legendary Skylander Spyro has qualities as rare as the race of magic purple dragons he descended from. A brave and headstrong hero, Spyro is always ready to use his Magic powers to scorch the forces of darkness. Spyro also has a brilliant mind—he has mastered the ability to access the powers of all the other elements, a skill that is unique to Spyro. His favorite element, other than Magic, is Fire. His enemies better watch out for his deadly flame breath!

"All Fired Up!"
SPYRO

Did you know?

Spyro has a photographic memory, which means he can remember objects and places in amazing detail. He knows all there is to know about Skylands.

MAGIC AURA

SLASHING TAIL

DARK DRAGON
There is a dark side to Spyro. He can channel the power of dark magic to transform into Dark Spyro, a fearsome foe with a shadowy edge. But Spyro must work hard to control his dark powers, otherwise the Darkness might consume him.

SHARP CLAWS

THE RUINS

Once a luscious, flourishing place, this mysterious, ancient island was home to the Core of Light. It was left devastated when the Core of Light was destroyed, and is now known as The Ruins. However, despite being reduced to rubble, The Ruins is still a magical place.

RIGHTY-O! LET'S FIND US A PLACE TO LAND.

THE DESTRUCTION

The Ruins was a vibrant citadel, home to Master Eon and the Skylanders (and some sheep). After the Core of Light exploded into pieces, everything here was immediately reduced to dust and rubble. All that was left was a pile of ruins... hence the name.

THE FAR-VIEWER

The Far-Viewer is a powerful telescope located in The Ruins. Looking through it shows the user the exact location of all the Eternal Sources. Helpful Hugo looks through it to reveal the location of the Eternal Sources to Skylanders. Sometimes it gets a bit rusty and needs to be oiled.

THE RESTORATION

Each component of the Core of Light must be restored for it to work again. As the brave Skylanders search for and find each of the Core of Light's Eternal Sources, The Ruins gradually becomes a lush and vibrant place to live again.

THE CORE OF LIGHT

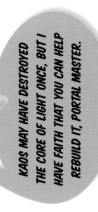

The Core of Light is vital to peace and balance in Skylands. Its beam of magical light is the only thing that can keep the Darkness, and evil, from spreading. Thanks to Kaos's actions, the pieces are scattered in the furthest reaches of Skylands. Now the Skylanders must find the pieces and restore the Core.

KAOS MAY HAVE DESTROYED THE CORE OF LIGHT ONCE, BUT I HAVE FAITH THAT YOU CAN HELP REBUILD IT, PORTAL MASTER.

MYSTERIOUS MACHINE

The Core of Light is as mysterious as it is powerful. It has protected Skylands for longer than anyone can remember and is said to have been built by the legendary Benevolent Ancients. Before it was destroyed, the machine's mysterious workings were always hidden by its domed roof. As the Ancients did not leave an instruction manual for it, rebuilding it could be hard!

EARTH
The Eternal Earth Source channels powerful energy through the Core. The Crystal Eye helps focus its power.

REBUILDING THE CORE

The Core of Light requires many different parts in order to shine once more and save Skylands. These pieces include the eight Eternal Elemental Sources. Each one provides the Core with a different power and energy, working in harmony to produce the machine's magical light. Each Source also requires a unique item to help harness its power. There is a lot to fit in!

AIR
Once the Eternal Air Source is returned to the Core, its powerful whirlwind draws in two Stone Guardians. These statues watch over the Core, and provide sturdy support for the rest of the pieces.

UNDEAD
The spooky Skull Mask provides a home for the Eternal Undead Source. It creates an eerie purple mist.

LIFE
Flowers bloom in the Core thanks to the Eternal Life Source. Green Goo of Primordia is also needed to grease the Core's gears.

FIRE
The Eternal Fire Source sits within the Crucible of the Ages. When both are added, the Core begins to glow. Things are hotting up!

TECH
The Eternal Tech Source drives the Golden Gear, an ancient mechanical wonder. The machine spins as its power builds.

WATER
The Eternal Water Source gushes through the Twin Spouts of Ocea-Major-Minor to drench the dry ground under the Core.

MAGIC
Quicksilver, a magical oil, and the Eternal Magic Source complete the Core. Together they activate the stunning beam of light.

UNDERGROUND
Beneath the Core of Light lie its foundations—a tangled mass of twisted roots and grinding gears. Machinery and nature work together in perfect harmony!

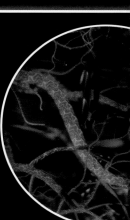

TUK'S EMPORIUM

Tuk's Emporium is a store located in Woodburrow. From treasures and charms to hats and maps, Tuk's Emporium has everything Portal Masters could need to make their Skylanders stronger, faster, and healthier. This handy catalog shows a selection of the items the store has on sale.

LEGENDARY TREASURES

Legendary Treasures are strange, weird, and sometimes wacky objects. These precious items will boost Skylanders' health, speed, or even give them some good luck to help them in battle.

BONNIE BONSAI

BOOMBOOM BOX

BUTTERING BLADE

MABU CARVING

BOG CHOWDER

CRUSTACEOUS CLOTHES

CHARMS

There's no harm in buying a charm. A charm gives the bearer special abilities, such as improved strength. Some special charms can even make Skylanders richer!

BONUS MAP

Keen for even more adventure? Perhaps you want to free a yeti stuck in an ice cream? Then Bonus Mission Maps are a great purchase! They transport Skylanders to hidden locations where they can carry out extra missions.

SINGING PUPPET

UNFORTUNATELY, NONE OF MY PRODUCTS CAN CLEAN MY STORE FOR ME.

HATS

Wearing hats is where it's at in Skylands, so cast your eyes over these magical millinery masterpieces. Purchasing one of these hats won't just make Skylanders look good—each hat has a different power to help the Skylander wearing it to get ahead of their enemies.

BIRTHDAY CAKE HAT

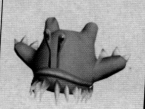

BITER HAT

BOTTLE CAP HAT

FLOWER HAT

DANGLING CARROT HAT

LAMPSHADE HAT

PANTS HAT

POLICE SIREN HAT

RASTA HAT

SHOWTIME HAT

TRAFFIC CONE HAT

UMBRELLA HAT

BACON BANDANA HAT

BOWLING PIN HAT

EARTH

The Earth element provides a strong and steady source of power for many Skylanders. It forms the foundations of Skylands itself, and can hide entire underground worlds. Earth is found in many forms, from the smallest speck of dirt to an enormous slab of rock.

ROCK 'N' ROLL

These Earth Skylanders are ready for more than just mud-slinging. They can manipulate minerals, crack open crystals, and shake the soil of Skylands in order to defeat their enemies. These powers make their foes quake with fear!

A REAL GEM

Some Earth Skylanders have the power to control crystals and precious gems. These heroes are not just interested in sparkling diamonds, though! Skylander Prism Break is a Rock Golem who shoots blinding beams of energy from the gleaming crystals in his arms.

SCORP

PRISM BREAK

FLASHWING

TERRAFIN

SLOBBER TOOTH

DOOM STONE

RUBBLE ROUSER

"It's Feeding Time!"

TERRAFIN

Did you know?

Terrafin used to live in the Dirt Seas with other Dirt Sharks. They all love swimming and snorkeling. Terrafin was the local lifeguard.

STREAMLINED FIN

KNUCKLE SPIKES

MUSCULAR ARMS

KNOCKOUT PUNCH
Terrafin is a very skilled boxer. The finned fighter's punch delivers bruising blows to his enemies. Terrafin is helped by his massive muscles and lethal metal boxing gloves.

TERRAFIN

As an ultra-strong and dynamic Dirt Shark, Terrafin has the ability to swim through earth! This means he can burrow underground and bypass his enemies. He then uses the element of surprise when he breaks through the surface, leaps high in the sky, and lands with a belly flop on whoever is in his way! Terrafin is very down-to-earth. He says what he thinks, and won't stand for nonsense!

MABU DEFENSE FORCE

The Mabu are a peaceful species found in villages throughout Skylands. These friendly creatures enjoy the quiet life and hate conflict. Yet troublesome Trolls, and the growing threat of evil, have forced them to take action. Enter the Mabu Defense Force—an army dedicated to defending the Mabu and their way of life.

HAVE NO FEAR, GENERAL ROBOT IS HERE

The MDF are ably assisted by General Robot. The most military-minded machine in Skylands has an endless supply of tactical advice to help the Defense Force in our struggles.

JOIN THE FIGHT AGAINST EVIL

The Mabu NEED YOU

MEEK AND MILD NO MORE!

Trampled by Trolls? Mad about Mabu mistreatment? Then join Captain Rizzo and the Mabu Defense Force! This brave Mabu is taking matters into his own paws by founding an army to fight against our foes. Rizzo is leading our well-drilled and disciplined Troll-bashing troops into battle. Don't delay, join the MDF today!

A PROVEN SUCCESS

It was the Mabu who rescued the Skylander, Prism Break, when he was trapped deep underground. The MDF carries on this bold tradition of bravery. We now count the Skylander as our closest ally.

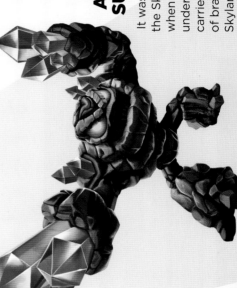

JOIN THE FORCE!

DON'T DELAY, JOIN TODAY!

☛ Go to your nearest Recruiting Station now!

FOLLOW IN FEARLESS FOOTSTEPS

Take inspiration from trailblazing Mabu like Flynn and Cali. This daring duo stand alongside the heroic Skylanders in the face of great evil. Just like them, you too could prove your Mabu mettle.

DECORATIVE SKULL

Some super strong Skylanders fight using one hundred percent pure muscle power! They use bare fists, brute force, and sheer body strength to beat, batter, and flatten opponents. Former boxing champion Night Shift sure knows how to knock out the enemy, sometimes with a single deadly punch.

HOW DO SKYLANDERS FIGHT?

A Skylander must be ready to leap into battle at a moment's notice. No two Skylanders have the same powers, but they are all fierce and gifted fighters. Each has a favorite fighting style and a set of skills linked to their elemental powers. Anything goes in a Skylander skirmish, from fists to fireballs!

SOME USE CUSTOM WEAPONS

Many Skylanders like to wield a weapon in battle, whether it be a sword, a blaster, or a crossbow. Some even have custom-made weapons designed for their special abilities. Roller Brawl loves competing with her roller derby team, so she found a novel way to combine her sport with being a Skylander—she has attached actual spinning blades to her boots.

ROTATING BLADE

SOME USE MAGIC

Some Skylanders use spells to dispel the enemy. Hoot Loop channels the Magic element to shoot powerful orbs from his staff. Even Skylanders with other elemental powers can use Magic. Life Skylander Zoo Lou uses it to summon animals to his side.

SOME MOVE AT AMAZING SPEEDS

Some Skylanders can run rings around their enemies and outwit their opponents with super-fast reactions. Freeze Blade skates at record-breaking speeds, on both ice and lava. In a fight, he throws his icy chakrams at top speed. Blink and you'll miss him!

SOME USE THEIR NATURAL POWER

ENERGY BEAM

Every species has its own natural strengths. Dragons are known for breathing fire in battle, but each dragon Skylander puts their own elemental twist on this talent. Camo breathes out a bright beam of pure energy, while Cynder fires dark lightning.

WHAT DOES IT TAKE TO BE A PILOT?

Soaring through the skies is a popular pastime in Skylands, but only the highest fliers have what it takes to become a pilot. With hazards to navigate, repairs to make, and sometimes unruly crews to manage, there is no chance of simply winging it! Flynn thinks he is "King of the Skies," but what is it that makes him so awesome (or not)?

AN AWESOME SHIP

Every pilot needs a ship. Ideally it should be fast, sleek, and full of the latest gadgets. Flynn's *Dread Yacht* may look like it is falling apart, but he prefers to describe it as "vintage." It is rumored in Skylands that this shabby ship is cursed, but Flynn has confidence in his trusty vessel.

Did you know?

A family of angry racoons once powered the engine on the *Dread Yacht*. Unrelated, calm raccoons would not have been able to power the ship. No one understands why this is.

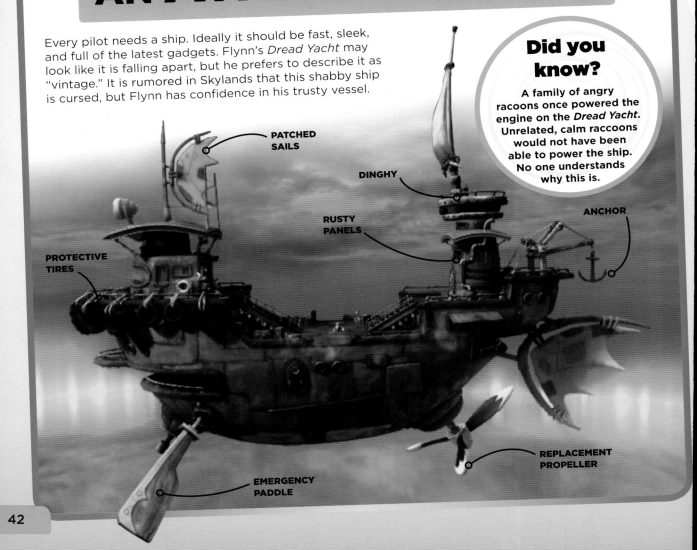

PATCHED SAILS

DINGHY

ANCHOR

RUSTY PANELS

PROTECTIVE TIRES

REPLACEMENT PROPELLER

EMERGENCY PADDLE

A GOOD CREW

Having a great crew on board makes for a successful voyage. Are they hardworking and loyal? Do they carry out repairs? Can they save the day when even the captain doesn't know what to do? Flynn's crew scores top marks!

A GOOD SENSE OF DIRECTION

Pilots need to have a natural sense of direction and should be experts with a map and compass. Getting lost is not an option! Flynn may struggle with his left and right, but he always finds his way in the end.

OPTIMISM

It's amazing how positive thinking can pull a ship through the narrowest of scrapes. A smiling pilot makes the ship a happy place to be and reassures nervous flyers like Hugo that everything is going well. Flynn has seen his fair share of trouble, but that doesn't worry him. He has bags of optimism and complete confidence in his "Flynn-stincts."

AN AWESOME POSE AND CATCHPHRASE

Flynn may not be the perfect pilot but he certainly looks the part. An amazing pose helps him show off his classic flying jacket and goggles. A matching catchphrase gives him the confidence of a captain. Flynn likes to tilt his body, stretch out his arms, and shout "Boom!"

I ALSO HAPPEN TO BE THE MOST HANDSOME PILOT IN SKYLANDS...

TRUSTED HANDS AT THE HELM

You will be personally welcomed onboard by your highly skilled and very confident captain, Flynn. Flynn has bags of piloting expertise and years of experience to help him navigate you safely through Skylands. With his engaging personality and winning smile, you may never want to leave!

DREAD YACHT TOURS

Do you dream of adventure? Do you yearn to visit the far-flung islands of Skylands while relaxing in total comfort? *Dread Yacht* Tours can make your dreams come true! Book the trip of a lifetime in this state-of-the-art cruiser, the *Dread Yacht*.

MEET THE CREW

You'll love getting to know our dedicated crew. Persephone, the ship's resident fairy, says, "The Mabu crew members are extremely helpful. They bring me shiny things, gems, and jewels."

ENJOY WONDERFUL ENTERTAINMENT

What could be more relaxing than listening to the sound of beautiful music as you glide through the sky? Our antique gramophone sound system plays all Captain Flynn's favorite songs. He doesn't take requests.

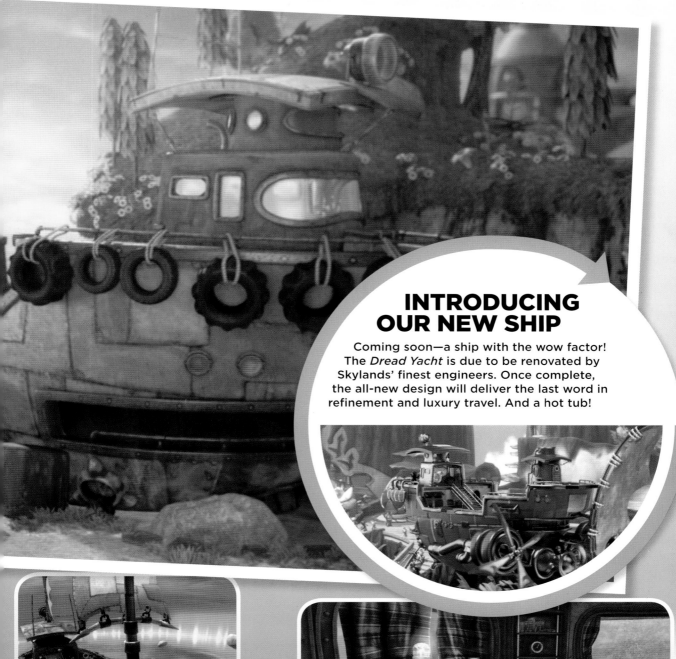

INTRODUCING OUR NEW SHIP

Coming soon—a ship with the wow factor! The *Dread Yacht* is due to be renovated by Skylands' finest engineers. Once complete, the all-new design will deliver the last word in refinement and luxury travel. And a hot tub!

VISIT HISTORIC SIGHTS

Step onto our detachable dinghy to visit some of Skylands' most beautiful and scenic locations, such as the Junkyard Isles and Motleyville. Captain Flynn will selflessly remain safely onboard to keep watch.

FIRST CLASS ACCOMMODATION

Our luxury cabins provide guests with the ultimate in airborne comfort. All rooms have a nautical style, and our most exclusive suites are furnished with authentic, working ship's machinery.

AIR

The Air element may be invisible but it is everywhere—in the sky, in the clouds, and in the breath of living creatures. Air normally drifts through Skylands creating a gentle breeze, but its power can be released in swirling storms and terrifying tornados!

AIR SQUADRON

Air Skylanders don't put up with airy-fairy nonsense. These dudes always deliver, whatever the weather. They fly at top speeds and control the skies by creating air blasts, starting storms, and whipping up whirling winds to blow their foes away.

STORMY SKIES

Skylands' residents are surrounded by clouds, so the weather is a major concern. Big tornados can cause serious damage, but smaller ones are quite popular. Mabu gather to throw stones, tax forms, and even sheep into the spiralling winds. Air Skylanders can often use their powers to control the weather.

JET-VAC

POP THORN

WHIRLWIND

WARNADO

SCRATCH

FREE RANGER

BOOM JET

"Hawk and Awe!"

JET-VAC

SKY BARON
HELMET

CLAWED
FINGERS

SNAPPING
BEAK

ARMORED
KNEE PADS

Did you know?

Jet-Vac is male but this Sky Baron Skylander has been known to lay eggs in times of shock. No one knows if these hatch into little Sky Barons or not...

JUMBO JET

Jet-Vac's versatile vacuum jets are not only used for flying. They also shoot fierce blasts of air that can deal a serious blow. If Jet-Vac hits reverse, enemies are pulled towards the spinning fan blades.

JET-VAC

Jet-Vac is a fearless flying ace and a master at maneuvering through the clouds—yet, amazingly, he is a wingless wonder. Years ago, this brave Sky Baron lost his wings while fighting evil. Master Eon was so impressed, he rewarded Jet-Vac's noble sacrifice with a special vacuum-powered jet pack. Now Jet-Vac carries this on his back instead of wings, and he flies just as high as ever. Jet-Vac has amazing eyesight, and always keeps watch over Skylands.

FLYING MACHINES

There are nearly as many airships in Skylands as there are sheep.* This handy Spotter's Guide gives the low-down on the differences between sleek and modern craft, huge old ships, and balloons blown at the mercy of the winds. It also provides warnings about some sinister ships that may be lurking in the clouds, so take care!

PIRATE SHIPS

Expect trouble if one of these scary ships docks nearby—villainous pirates stand ready to fire cannon balls from the deck. These vessels can negotiate both water and air, so there is no escape!

Spotter's Notes:

I bet these swashbuckling ships are full of treasure! Shame about the skull decorations, though.

Spotter's Score: 6/10

ALL-RIGHTY! I'VE RUN INTO LOADS OF SHIPS ON MY ADVENTURES SO I'VE ADDED MY OWN NOTES AND SCORES. NOTHING BEATS AN EXPERT'S OPINION!

HOT AIR BALLOON

A hot air balloon is the most graceful way to travel. With expert piloting, you can drift gently or speed through Skylands. They aren't easy to steer though, so be prepared to go where the wind takes you!

Spotter's Notes:

Ah, my old reliable balloon! Perfect for picnics, but not so good in a fight.

Spotter's Score: 5/10

*There is no Spotter's Guide for sheep. They all look the same.

SHARPFIN'S AIRSHIP

This ultra-fast, streamlined airship comes in handy for Skylands residents who need to make a quick getaway. With multiple propellers, high-tech equipment, and custom paint work, this is an expensive ship to own.

Spotter's Notes:

This ship is almost as awesome as the *Dread Yacht* (but don't tell the old girl I said that).

Spotter's Score: 9/10

ARKEYAN ROBOT

This Arkeyan Robot was frozen in ice for an age before the Skylanders recovered it. It is a huge haunted robot with the power of flight. This magnificent machine shoots lasers from its eyes and has crushing fists.

Spotter's Notes:

A flying robot with laser eyes?! BOOM!

Spotter's Score: 10/10

ARKEYAN COPTER

Arkeyan Copters, also known as Arkeyan Autogyros, were formally used by the Arkeyans to defend their territory. A few of these remnants of the ancient civilization still remain in Skylands. The craft's three rotary blades allow them to both fly and hover in place.

Spotter's Notes:

The Arkeyans may have been pretty evil, but they really knew how to make a machine.

Spotter's Score: 8/10

DROW ZEPPELIN

A combination of balloon and propeller moves this Drow Zeppelin through the clouds. Used by crafty Drow elves as a warship, this cannon-firing craft is one to watch out for. The evil elves can stash away in the ship's hold, ready to attack.

Spotter's Notes:

I like the bright colors but these Drow ships give me the creeps.

Spotter's Score: 7/10

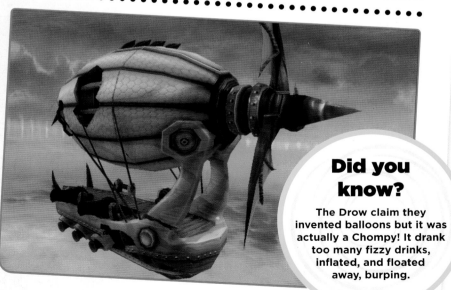

Did you know?

The Drow claim they invented balloons but it was actually a Chompy! It drank too many fizzy drinks, inflated, and floated away, burping.

Trolls LOVE explosives. They think any problem can be solved by the application of lots of dynamite. Grenadier Trolls throw powerful explosives and use long-range weapons to blast their enemies away.

GRENADIER

WITH EXPLOSIVES

BLASTER

HOW DO TROLLs FIGHT?

The Trolls are Kaos's most loyal soldiers. They are nasty pieces of work, whose main hobbies include war, drilling for oil, and chopping down forests. These brutal beasts are skilled engineers, but only ever use their talents for evil. They have created a huge range of weapons and vehicles for fighting enemies.

WITH MELEE WEAPONS

Trolls aren't afraid to get their hands dirty. Maces, wrenches, and claws all make effective weapons for close-range battles. Some Trolls also wear metal armor to protect them in hand-to-hand combat.

MACE MAJOR

TROLLVERINE

GREASE MONKEY

WITH VEHICLES

The Trolls' vehicles are designed to do many different jobs in battle. Chainsaw Tanks make short work of destroying forests, Mark 31 Tanks can fire barrages of rockets, and Gun Snout mechs can trample all over their enemies. All of them make huge amounts of pollution.

CHAINSAW TANK

MARK 31 TANK

GUN SNOUT

Did you know?

Trolls like to play fetch with Chompies. They throw lit dynamite for them to catch. They call this game

BOOM!

WITH A SUPER TANK

Watch out for the Trolls' Super Tank. The Trolls have brought it to the battlefield to fight against the Mabu Defense Force. Its huge gun and whirling blades make it a very dangerous opponent.

FIRE

From the molten lava that fills the deepest volcano to the flame of a birthday candle, the ancient Fire element is found throughout Skylands. Emitting sizzling heat and radiant light, the power of Fire is a sight to behold, but don't get too close!

ELEMENTAL GATES

Only a Fire Skylander can pass through Fire Elemental Gates. These magical doorways open to reveal hidden vaults and top secret places. Other Skylanders can pass through their own Elemental Gates but they will never uncover the secrets that the Fire Gates guard.

FIRE FIGHTERS

Holy smoke! With talents ranging from breathing flames to throwing bombs, Skylanders with the power of Fire can be way too hot to handle. Some Fire Skylanders wield blazing weapons, including arrows, axes, and whips. These guys will set fire to anything they can get their hands on.

FRYNO

SMOLDERDASH

ERUPTOR

HOT DOG

BLAST ZONE

FIRE KRAKEN

"Born to Burn!"

ERUPTOR

Did you know?

Eruptor used to live with other lava creatures until the day a heated argument broke out at a lava-pool party. The pressure caused their volcano to explode and they were all scattered across Skylands.

BLAZING
EYES

HOT HEAD

BARELY
CONTAINED HEAT

MOLTEN
LAVA

ERUPTOR

Lava monster Eruptor was born underground inside a volcano. Like all of his kind, Eruptor naturally has a very short fuse and can sometimes literally erupt with anger about something—whether it be Kaos trying to destroy Skylands or a squeaky floorboard. However, over time, the cool air in Skylands has helped Eruptor learn to control his inner fire, and he tries to only truly unleash it against evil forces.

HOT-HEADED
Eruptor has a habit of spitting or hurling scorching balls of pure magma at his foes. If these burning blobs don't fry his opponents, Eruptor can transform himself into an entire pool of molten lava.

ARE THE CYCLOPES SCARY?

Cyclopses come in different forms—they can be big or small, strong or weak. All of them, however, have a single beady eye to spot strangers with. These bad beasts are far from sociable—if they spy any outsiders, they will attack them, making these unfriendly creatures a real nuisance for Skylanders. Kaos often enlists their help in his schemes, but are Cyclopses really all that scary?

YES, THEY LOOK SCARY

The major thing that makes Cyclopses scary is the fact that they look scary. Let's face it, if you see a creature with one staring eyeball and two super-sharp fangs running towards you, you are going to be scared. Very scared indeed. Aren't you running yet?

YES, THEY HAVE SCARY ANIMALS

As if the Cyclopses themselves aren't scary-looking enough, their pet animals are a whole new level of scary. Take, for example, the disgusting Slobbering Mutticus. It will spit gooey green slime at you whilst clawing you. Then there's the mutant Cyclops Mammoth. It's so out of control that it has to be chained up at all times. If it breaks free, it will trample on you!

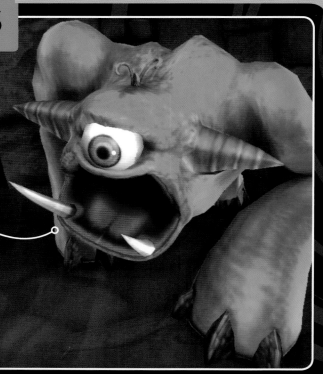

CYCLOPS MAMMOTH

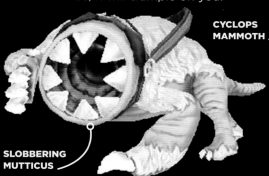

SLOBBERING MUTTICUS

NO, THEY ARE NOT VERY BRAVE

Cyclopses prefer safety in numbers and hardly ever battle alone. While some varieties of Cyclopses don't think twice about taking on a foe, these Timidclopses do. When they run out of big barrels to roll at enemies, these wimps quickly look for a hiding place to cower in or the nearest cliff to jump off! Anything is better than coming eye-to-eye with an enemy.

NO, THEY ARE NOT VERY CLEVER

Cyclopses are all eyeball and little brain. They have some talents in stonemasonry, but their attempts to make stone boats and balloons have always sunk without a trace. Cyclops Choppers are ax-wielding critters. When they see a stranger, they start spinning their axes at great speeds. Sure, this looks impressive, but Choppers forget that it makes them very, very dizzy.

YES, THEY ARE SMELLY

Cyclopses have an aversion to bathing, so you will most likely smell them before you see them. These Mohawk Cyclopses take pride in their hair, but they have the same pungent odor as every other kind of Cyclops!

RETURN OF THE GIANTS

Some 10,000 years ago, there lived eight Giants who were the very first Skylanders. These legendary heroes saved Skylands from the evil Arkeyans. Now a new threat is looming in the shape of Portal Master Kaos, Skylands needs their help once more.

THE GIANTS WERE ONCE THOUGHT TO BE THE STUFF OF LEGEND.

EYE-BRAWL

The formidable Eye-Brawl was created when a headless giant and a flying eyeball decided to join forces after fighting in an epic battle that lasted 100 years. This Undead Giant always has his eye on the prize—it's quite a sight when the eye detaches itself and shoots lasers, while the fists throw furious punches.

CRUSHER

Earth Giant Crusher isn't fussy when it comes to rocks—big ones, small ones, and everything in between—he always has a smashing time pulverizing them into tiny fragments with his massive hammer. He also crushes his enemies to smithereens with the same level of love and attention. For Crusher, every hour is crush hour!

NINJINI

Ninjini has a lot of bottle. In fact, the ninja genie was actually trapped in one by a jealous sorceress for centuries. But through sheer strength and determination, the Magic Giant managed to escape. Everyone who comes up against Ninjini wishes they could beat her in a duel, but with her magical mix of skill, sorcery, and swordplay, it's not easy!

TREE REX

Terrifying Life Giant Tree Rex was once a magnificent, peaceful tree until pollution from an Arkeyan factory turned him into a moving mutant. He uses his tree-mendous strength to charge at enemies and batter and flatten them. Tree Rex's foes should definitely be afraid of his bark!

HOT HEAD

When Hot Head bathed in a pool of magic oil to cool down one day, he gained an infinite fuel supply! Now, anything and anyone that gets in his way faces his fiery wrath. The hot-tempered Fire Giant can hurl roaring flame blasts and flammable oil blobs at will.

SWARM

Air Giant Swarm had a massive growth spurt and was forced to leave his hive home. He soon found his place in the world when he was discovered by the other Giants. The brilliant bee uses his vicious sting to give lethal barbed attacks against foes. But he gets his biggest buzz of all when he transforms into a hive full of angry, stinging bees!

BOUNCER

Tech robot Bouncer used to be an All-Star Roboto Ball player. But when the Arkeyans outlawed the game, bulky Bouncer decided to join the Giants and use his gaggle of gadgets to attack his enemies. His laser-shooting eyes and rocket launcher shoulders make Bouncer the wheel deal.

THUMPBACK

Ex-pirate Thumpback has a whale of a time catching fish, but he also loves to net the forces of evil. The sea-faring Water Giant swings his anchor and attacks enemies with whale-sized chomps. His awesome belly flop attack also creates some mighty waves and causes serious damage.

DISCOVER THE ARKEYANS

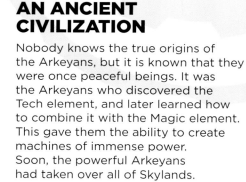

Who exactly were the ancient Arkeyans? Unfortunately, much of their history has been lost. What we do know is that the influence of this ancient civilization continues to be felt in Skylands today, and lots of their inventions and discoveries still live on, many years since their reign ended.

INVENTORS

The Arkeyans were brilliant inventors. Using the Tech element, they created ugly machines of war and a race of colossal security robots. These robots had a range of mighty powers to keep the inhabitants of Skylands in slavery.

AN ANCIENT CIVILIZATION

Nobody knows the true origins of the Arkeyans, but it is known that they were once peaceful beings. It was the Arkeyans who discovered the Tech element, and later learned how to combine it with the Magic element. This gave them the ability to create machines of immense power. Soon, the powerful Arkeyans had taken over all of Skylands.

ARKEYAN WAR MACHINES

ANCIENT ARKEYAN PLATFORM

LOST CITY

The Lost City of Arkus was the center of the Arkeyan civilization. Some 10,000 years ago, the Giants joined forces to free Skylands from the grip of the Arkeyan King and his armies. The Giants destroyed the Arkeyans, but the remnants of their civilization can still be found in Skylands.

FIST OF ARKUS

Constructed from Tech and Magic elements, the Iron Fist of Arkus can bring to life and control the entire Arkeyan robot army. If a non-robotic being wears the fist, they are transformed into a huge robot. The fist has been a source of conflict throughout history because of the power it carries—everyone wants to get their hands on it!

SPIKED EPAULETS

CHOP CHOP

Chop Chop is proof that not everything from the Arkeyan empire is bad. The elite Undead warrior had an encounter with Master Eon, resulting in Chop Chop switching over to the good side. Now this Skylander uses his savvy swordplay and shield skills to chop down the forces of evil!

ANCIENT ARKEYAN BLADE

LEARN ABOUT ALL THINGS ARKEYAN. WELL, THE BITS I KNOW, ANYWAY...

THE ARKEYAN CONQUERTRON

LETHAL LASER EYES

The Conquertron is a massive ancient robot with terrifying levels of strength. It towers over virtually all creatures and easily conquers anything in its path. The Conquertron was built by the Arkeyans many ages ago, but now it's under Kaos's control—and as usual, the pint-sized Portal Master plans to use it to do something stupendously nasty...

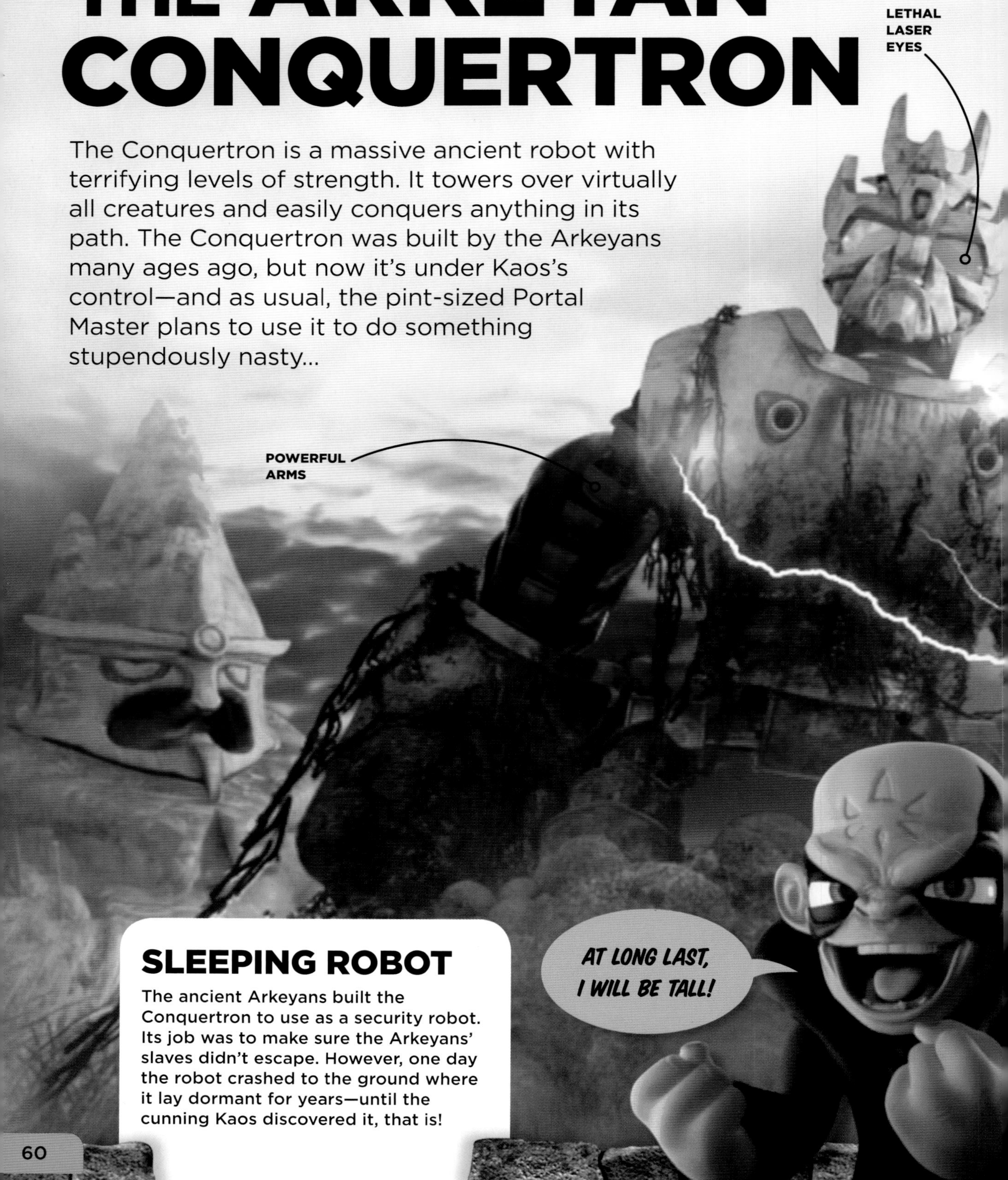

POWERFUL ARMS

SLEEPING ROBOT

The ancient Arkeyans built the Conquertron to use as a security robot. Its job was to make sure the Arkeyans' slaves didn't escape. However, one day the robot crashed to the ground where it lay dormant for years—until the cunning Kaos discovered it, that is!

AT LONG LAST, I WILL BE TALL!

EVIL PLANS

With the robot under his power, Kaos quickly realizes he can use its mighty strength to search for the Iron Fist of Arkus—an ancient object that can control an entire army of Arkeyan robots. Kaos hopes to use the power of the Iron Fist to help him take over Skylands.

STAIRWAY TO DOMINATION

When Kaos crash-landed near the Conquertron, the energy from the impact accidentally triggered the Conquertron's start-up sequence, bringing the vast robot back to life.

COCKPIT CONTROL

The robot's cockpit is located behind its eyes. Kaos and his butler Glumshanks can control the Conquertron's every movement from it.

CONQUERING CONQUERTRON

The Conquertron can shoot powerful lasers from its eyes and arms. It can also smash and trample anything that gets in its way with the might of its enormous metallic body.

MOSS FROM
LAYING DORMANT

TECH

The power of the Tech element is reflected in the might of machines and robotic creatures. The Arkeyans first discovered how to harness Tech, and used it to engineer awesome inventions for their empire. Complicated Tech machines require masterful mechanics to keep them in good working order.

TECH TEAM

Those with the Tech element have a natural affinity for machines and gizmos. These high-tech warriors all have the weaponry needed to destroy evil, and some are even fully fledged robots! Tech is about more than just flicking a switch, though. These guys are full of courage, talent, and drive.

GOLDEN GEAR

As this ancient and mysterious device grinds and turns, it helps Skylands to run like clockwork. The powerful Golden Gear drives every clever contraption and cunning machine that uses Tech. Nothing mechanical would function without it, from engines to record players.

TRIGGER HAPPY

SPROCKET

COUNTDOWN

WIND-UP

MAGNA CHARGE

SPY RISE

"The Fix is in!"

SPROCKET

Did you know?

The Golding species are famous for being rich and living in luxury. Sprocket is not interested in such fancy things, however, and prefers to be in her lab.

WELDING
GOGGLES

WRENCH

CUSTOM-
MADE ARMOR

SPROCKET

As a genius inventor and mechanic, Sprocket mends machinery with ease. As a Skylander, she can also leave her evil enemies in a fix! This gadget-mad Golding has even assembled her own high-tech battle suit. Sprocket inherited her love of inventing from her uncle, but when he mysteriously disappeared, Sprocket knew Kaos was to blame. She dedicated her energy to becoming a Skylander, fighting evil, and finding her uncle.

TURRET TERROR
Sprocket's favorite gadget is her gun turret, where she sits and shoots at enemies. It even turns into a moving assault tank. When on foot, Sprocket is armed with a huge heavy-duty wrench. She really puts a spanner in the works of any evil plans!

As a Portal Master, Master Eon is always searching for worthy individuals to become Skylanders. Being a Skylander requires skill, courage, and loyalty. Not everyone is cut out for the job! Answer Eon's questions and find out who in Skylands you are most similar to, and whether or not you have what it takes to fight alongside the Skylanders.

COULD YOU BE A SKYLANDER?

ARE YOU ADVENTUROUS AND WILLING TO TAKE RISKS?

YES →

Do people look to you as a leader?

NO

Do you spend your time eating and staring at clouds?

YES

NO

Have you ever developed a top-secret, dastardly plan to take over Skylands for your own gain?

NO →

PORTAL MASTER

Your wisdom exceeds your physical strength, and you always see the best in creatures. Forget being a Skylander, you should be picking them like Eon does!

YES

KAOS

You are as troublesome as Kaos is! The Skylanders have enough evil to fight without another evil genius showing up.

YES

YES →

SKYLANDER

Brave, strong, and good—you have all the qualities required to make an excellent Skylander. Keep up the good work!

Have you got a strong sense of elemental power?

NO →

HANDY HELPER

Not everyone protects Skylands on the battlefields! Like Hugo and Flynn, your kind heart and useful skills would make you a brilliant guide for a Skylander.

 NO   **YES**

MINION

Mean and cowardly residents of Skylands often end up as minions of Kaos. If you don't want to follow in their footsteps, maybe you should try being a little kinder.

Do you always try to do good and help your friends?

NO →

SHEEP

Sheep are found all over Skylands but they are never particularly helpful. Maybe you aren't cut out for fighting evil.

DISTANT REALMS

No one knows where Skylands begins and ends, so it's full of remote kingdoms, all waiting to be discovered. However, some of these far-flung corners are feeling the influence of the Darkness. Rotten rulers, marauding monsters, and vile villains are spreading their power...

PIE STORE

THE DRAGON'S THRONE

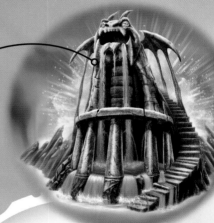

DARKLIGHT CRYPT

This is a spooky place where the Undead are out of control. The Undead lived happily alongside the living here until a giant Eyeball Monster moved to the island. Now, Occulous forces the Undead to do evil things, like eating brains instead of pie!

ENTER IF YOU DARE!

DRAGON'S PEAK

For centuries, Dragon's Peak was a peaceful land. It was ruled by the rightful king, Ramses, from the Dragon's Throne. But Vathek, Ramses' evil brother, turned Ramses to stone and now Vathek and his minions rule ruthlessly over the land's creatures.

ICE FALL

EMPIRE OF ICE

The village of Vindlevale was a sunny paradise until chilling Ice Ogres moved in. The Ice Ogres built a massive wall to block out the sun. Now, the icy grip of an endless winter hangs over these snowy wastelands.

CROW'S NEST

PIRATE SEAS

Located within the Pirate Seas, Coconut Island is occupied by dastardly pirates. Each time the beastly buccaneers cheat and win another card game, they take an islander prisoner. Now there are hardly any islanders left who are free.

CANNON

WATER

The Water element flows abundantly in Skylands. It is central to the undersea kingdoms and frozen ice realms that many creatures call home. Elsewhere, it is present in pools, rivers, and seas. It is also found in the bodies of most living things, and is critical for survival.

MAKING WAVES

Water Skylanders are always making a splash with their wide range of special powers. These watery warriors can summon waves to wash away opponents, freeze enemies in ice, and summon sea creatures to use in starfish bullets and swordfish attacks.

WATERY WORLDS

Water supports many undersea species. Lots of these creatures live their whole lives beneath the waves, and are unaware of the world above the surface. Water Skylanders are well suited to fighting when water is near. Often gifted swimmers, they are not afraid of getting wet!

WHAM-SHELL

PUNK SHOCK

RIP TIDE

CHILL

WASH BUCKLER

GILL GRUNT

FREEZE BLADE

"Fear the Fish!"

GILL GRUNT

DORSAL
FIN

Did you know?

Gill Grunt trained in the Gillmen Marines, the toughest force in the watery world. It was on his first mission that he discovered the cloudy world beyond his undersea home.

SCALY SKIN

LEATHER
WRIST GUARDS

WEBBED FEET

HARPOON

GILL GRUNT

Gill Grunt is one of the longest serving Skylanders. This fiercely loyal and courageous Gillman will stop at nothing to defeat evil. Gill has buckets of special water gadgets to help him, including a powerful water cannon and a hose which sprays bubbling, boiling water. He speeds around Skylands using a water jet pack, as he searches for a mysterious mermaid he fell in love with many years ago.

HARMFUL HARPOON
Gill Grunt is an ace shot with his harpoon gun. If he really wants to show off, Gill can even shoot three harpoon darts from his gun at once, making it triple-tricky for his evil enemies to escape from his awesome aim!

ERRR... WHY DID I AGREE TO BRING YOU HERE AGAIN? BEST NOT HANG AROUND FOR LONG!

DOMAINS OF KAOS

Every good villain needs a secret hiding place and Kaos is no exception! After each humiliating defeat by the Skylanders, he likes to head home. Hidden away in the darkest corners of his Kastle and protected by a staff of nasty minions, Kaos can plot his next move!

KAOS'S KASTLE

Kaos adores his spooky Kastle. Its gloomy interiors, secret passages, and ultra-secure ramparts provide him with the perfect stronghold. This is where Kaos grew up, but it's no happy home. Kaos's Mom often visits, and she is even more evil than him. She is always scheming with her monstrous friends at dinner parties Kaos isn't invited to.

LAIR OF KAOS

Perfect for an evil genius on-the-go, Kaos's lair is a terrifying flying fortress packed full of perilous traps! Frightening spiked fangs line its dark paths and terrible monsters lie in wait, ready to pounce! It takes a brave Skylander to dare to enter it.

SHEER WALLS

TACKY TASTE
Kaos isn't subtle in his choice of decorations. The egotistical overlord has filled his home with statues and portraits of his own ugly image! It reminds Kaos, and everybody else, exactly who's boss. His butler, Glumshanks, has the unfortunate job of polishing and dusting every single one.

PROTECTIVE
SHIELD
GENERATOR

KAOS'S EVIL LAB
Deep in the Kastle's dungeons, where he cannot be disturbed, Kaos dreams up new ways to defeat the Skylanders. This is also where he can try out his malicious magic and sinister inventions. Poor Glumshanks normally provides a convenient test subject for Kaos's extreme experiments!

TIDY FRONT
GARDEN

SWAP FORCE

WASH BUCKLER

Pirate Wash Buckler is a Water Skylander. His eight tentacles come in handy for wielding both a bubble gun and a deadly cutlass.

BLAST ZONE

This Furnace Knight has a blast playing with fire. Whether Blast Zone is throwing bombs or breathing flames, the results are always explosive.

BOOM JET

Boom Jet loves to sky-surf through the air, but he's no laid-back surfer dude. He hurls his huge football bombs with lethal accuracy!

DOOM STONE

This Earth Skylander is carved out of strong stone. When he brandishes his club and shield, there's a definite sense of doom!

STINK ZONE

Stink Zone is a combo of bad smells, ninja prowess, and lightning speed—a fusion of foul odors and fast rocket dashes that proves deadly!

WASH JET

Wash Buckler's sword skills are even more dangerous flying through the sky on Boom Jet's sky surfer. This jumbled hero displays real flair in the air.

BLAST STONE

Blending Blast Zone's mighty bombs and fiery breath with Doom Stone's special spin kicks creates Blast Stone—a highly explosive mix!

BOOM CHARGE

When Boom Charge whizz around on his wheel it give him extra speed to throw football bombs further, faster, and harder!

The SWAP Force is an elite band of Skylanders who are a force to be reckoned with! When they were caught in a blast from the magical volcano, Mount Cloudbreak, they gained the power to swap halves and combine their talents.

MAGNA CHARGE

This Tech Skylander's magnetic head gives him a magnetic personality. With cannon and pick-up powers, he attracts and repels!

HOOT LOOP

Mighty magician Hoot Loop is an owl who always has a trick under his wing. His magical powers and portal make him a feathered force.

NIGHT SHIFT

Undead vampire boxer Night Shift packs a massive punch with his skull gloves. His deadly vampire fangs have a lot of bite, too!

STINK BOMB

Life Skylander Stink Bomb releases vile vapors that no nose can cope with! A skilled ninja, his martial arts abilities are the bomb.

DOOM LOOP

Doom Loop combines Doom Stone's weaponry for attack and Hoot Loop's portal ring—powers that help him run rings around his foes.

MAGNA SHIFT

Magna Shift uses smash-and-grab battle tactics. His top half delivers a blast of magnet cannon, then his bottom half teleports him away.

HOOT BOMB

Combining Hoot Loop's owl sorcery and Stink Bomb's skunk-fu skills makes for one mighty mash-up! Hoot Bomb is tricky for enemies to defeat.

NIGHT BUCKLER

Night Buckler's terrifying tentacles allow him to deliver an even bigger boxing punch. It's a knock-out combination!

CLOUDBREAK ISLANDS

The Cloudbreak Islands are magical, mysterious places, full of wonder, adventure, and history. At their center is a magical volcano, Mount Cloudbreak, where the SWAP Force were created. All types of terrain can be found here, from marshland and deserts to forests and wintry wastelands. Unfortunately, wherever there is powerful magic in Skylands, there is also great danger...

THIS JUST DOESN'T FEEL NATURAL. WHERE'S THE PROPELLER?

WOODBURROW

Woodburrow is the busiest village in the Cloudbreak Islands. Friendly inhabitants such as Rufus the town crier will always welcome Skylanders here, and it makes a great place for weary travelers to rest. In the center of the village is a mysterious pool from where, it is said, a wizard was once transported to another world, so nobody is allowed to swim there anymore.

MOUNT CLOUDBREAK

The legendary Mount Cloudbreak erupts once every one hundred years, replenishing the magic throughout Skylands. It is here that the SWAP Force Skylanders were formed. They were tasked with protecting the Cloudbreak Islands and the volcano from evil forces. But during an epic battle, they got caught in the volcano's eruption and the magic energy from the blast gave the Skylanders the ability to swap their powers—and bodies!

THE AIRDOCKS

The Airdocks is where visiting airships touring the Cloudbreak Islands can moor up and get some much-needed repairs or a lick of paint. Flynn's ship, the *Dread Yacht*, is transformed from a rust bucket to all kinds of awesome here. Updates to Flynn's ship include a spy mode switch and a hot tub!

LIFE

The Life element flows through all living things in Skylands, and is ever-present in the world of nature. Life's elemental power provides balance and harmony in Skylands. Life is also incredibly resilient and can survive in the harshest of conditions.

GREEN TEAM

Life Skylanders are a true force of nature. Some of these Skylanders use their elemental powers to create weapons out of plants. This can mean throwing exploding fruit, shooting spiny seeds, or battering opponents with enormous tree stump fists. Other Life Skylanders employ animal assistance in their battles against evil.

THE TREE OF LIFE

This forest realm is known by most in Skylands as Treetop Terrace, but its Tree Folk inhabitants call it "The Tree of Life." The Life element is teeming here, in both the landscape and its residents. Life Skylanders are reinvigorated when they visit and their powers are strengthened.

STEALTH ELF

BUMBLE BLAST

ZOO LOU

CAMO

STINK BOMB

GRILLA DRILLA

POINTY
ELF EARS

Did you know?

There are many elves found in Skylands, including some mean ones. Elves who have turned evil are called Drow. They still retain their love of nature and gardening, when they aren't causing trouble.

"Silent but Deadly!"

STEALTH ELF

RAZOR
SHARP
BLADE

NINJA MASK

SOFT-SOLED
SHOES

STEALTH ELF

From birth, Stealth Elf's life has always been entwined with nature. She has no knowledge of her family or origins before she was found in the forest by a mysterious ninja. He became Stealth Elf's mentor and taught her how to protect her woodland home. This sneaky Skylander can create a decoy version of herself to distract her enemies, while she becomes invisible and slips past them.

DAGGER DANGER
Stealth Elf's training taught her how to use a variety of intimidating weapons. Cyclopses are no match for this nature-loving ninja!

Everyone in Skylands knows that pirates are a terrifying bunch. Amongst this horrible lot, pirate captains are the most vicious and powerful pirates of all. These infamous seafarers are even feared by their own crews. Nobody wants a close shave with either Captain Frightbeard or Captain Dreadbeard, the two most blood-thirsty buccaneers.

THEY ARE SCARY

CAPTAIN DREADBEARD

CAPTAIN FRIGHTBEARD

WHAT MAKES A PIRATE?

Pirate ships ride both the waves and the clouds in Skylands, which makes them a constant threat. Pirates are always ready to weigh anchor and cause mayhem. They are traditionally from seadog or squid-like species, but all kinds of creatures are welcome to join these bandits-in-boats!

THEY ARE PART OF A CREW

Look out for these tough gangs! Pirates are loyal to their captain and will always defend their shipmates against a rival crew. That's why pirates spend more time fighting each other than they do causing trouble on land.

SEADOG PIRATES

CAPTAIN K9S

SEADOG SKIPPERS

SQUIDDLERS

THEY SCHEME

Pirates are always planning scams to earn some gold. From treasure hunting to plundering villages, the swashbuckling scoundrels will do anything to get some loot. Pirates even kidnapped Gill Grunt's mermaid girlfriend for a ransom! They never get rich though, as they gamble all their gold away playing Skystones.

Did you know?

Skystones is a popular game in Skylands. It was invented by lazy Molekin builders. They got bored with tiling and started playing with the tiles instead.

CUTLASS

TENTACLES

WASH BUCKLER

THEY CAN BECOME SKYLANDERS

Not all pirates are cruel and nasty. Some ex-pirates have reformed and want to make amends for their misdemeanors. Both Wash Buckler and Thumpback renounced ruthlessness. These sailors are now Skylanders dedicated to doing good.

ANCHOR

THUMPBACK

BARNACLES

BLASTANEERS

SQUIDFACE BRUTES

UNDEAD

The Undead element has a bit of a bad reputation. It is certainly creepy, with its close links to evil, the Darkness, and the Underworld. But the Undead element is a vital component of the Core of Light, and the Undead Skylanders are all good ghouls and ghosts!

THE UNDERWORLD

The Underworld is a dangerous place, full of evil Undead creatures. Those who visit the Underworld risk becoming a member of the Undead forever. Count Moneybone, Lord of the Underworld, is the worst of its residents. He wants to extend his bony grip across the whole of Skylands.

GHOSTLY GANG

Spooky Skylanders use the power of the Undead element to keep evil at bay. In fact, these haunted heroes are dead good at it! Between them, they can summon spooks, unleash vampire claws, and make it rain skulls. These scary tactics both fight and frighten foes.

ROLLER BRAWL

CHOP CHOP

GRIM CREEPER

CYNDER

NIGHT SHIFT

RATTLE SHAKE

"Volts and Lightning!"
CYNDER

Did you know?

Cynder doesn't enjoy pranks or jokes of any kind. The Skylander Wrecking Ball once tried to trip Cynder up with his long tongue. Cynder zapped him with lightning and he could not eat for two weeks!

SPIKED WING TIPS

VAST WINGS

POWERFUL TAIL

LIGHTNING BREATH

CYNDER

Mysterious dragoness Cynder is a Skylander with a dark past. She was raised by a cruel dragon master named Malefor and forced to do his evil bidding. Fellow Skylander Spyro helped free Cynder from Malefor, and she is now committed to saving Skylands from dark forces. Cynder works hard to keep her sinister side at bay, but the other Skylanders still find her a little scary!

DARK LIGHTNING
Cynder's specialty is breathing high-voltage bolts of dark lightning to shock her enemies. Cynder also has the power to take on a shadowy form when she needs to escape.

GHOSTS AND GHOULS

There are many Undead enemies who roam Skylands causing heaps of trouble with their horrible hauntings. These creepy creatures are full of frightful ways to scare and attack the living. Often using the element of surprise, these supernatural pests fight with a scary determination!

ROTTING ROBBIES

Rotting Robbies are zombies who bite, swipe, and snack on the brains of the living. It takes a lot to stop these decomposing dummies in their tracks, even when their limbs start to drop off!

EYEBALL STILL INTACT... JUST.

LARGE HAND FOR SWIPING

TROG WANDERERS

Trog Wanderers are weird beings that move around very slowly. However, if anyone attacks these nasties, they get smaller and faster. The shrunken beasts then run straight at their attacker and try to give them a nasty bite.

Did you know?

The living fear the Undead, but the Undead can't understand why. After all, the living and the Undead will all be on the same team eventually!

RHU-BARBS

The Rhu-Barbs are summoned from another dimension by Undead Spell Punks to carry out the most ferocious of attacks. With their razor-sharp knife arms and pointy teeth, these savage monsters can do some serious damage.

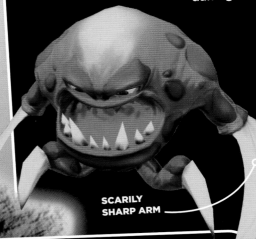

SCARILY
SHARP ARM

GHOSTS

These ghoulish ghosts aren't particularly ghastly. They used to feed on the brains of the living, but they changed their dietary habits when they discovered a liking for pies. For them, nothing compares to tasty pastry. This Machine Ghost is actually quite a sensitive soul—it haunts an Arkeyan robot, but not in a very scary way.

BONE 'N' ARROWS

Bone 'n' Arrows are exactly that—bones with arrows! Despite having no eyes, these spine-chilling skeletons are able to fire their longbows with amazing accuracy. They also have an annoying habit of cackling whenever they fire a shot!

BONY
LONGBOW

SHADOW KNIGHTS

These living suits of armor stand very still and patiently wait for their victims to pass. Then, they suddenly spring to life and launch a surprise attack. The Shadow Knights lash out with their swords but they also have another trick up their plated sleeves: Their swords release deadly electricity bolts.

SHINING
ARMOR

FLORA AND FAUNA

Skylands is swarming with amazing animals and vibrant vegetation. Travel around this nature trail to familiarize yourself with Skylands' wildlife, its frozen wastelands, and its boggy swamps. But be careful—some of the beasts you will encounter are pretty nasty!

BOGHOGS

Marshland

The Boghogs live deep in the muddy marshlands of Skylands. These swamp-dwelling boars never get bored of squelching around in a bog. Some water-dwelling Gillmen keep Boghogs as companions.

SHEEP

The sheep like to graze peacefully on the pastures of Skylands. These balls of fluff are thought to be harmless, but a certain Mabu (Hugo) might disagree. The mean Geargolems pick on the sheep and have been known to use the poor things as ammunition!

SUGARBATS

With their big eyes and ears, Sugarbats are as sweet as, well, sugar. But be wary of the Evilized Sugarbats. They have turned sour and don't bat an eyelid when it comes to attacking anything that moves.

SPIDER SWARMERS

Watch out for these creepy critters. Spider Swarmers scuttle around in huge swarms. As soon as they spot an enemy, they storm straight for it and explode in a toxic green cloud, ending their own lives and possibly a Skylander's life, too.

Pastureland

Snowland

CHILLYDOGS

There are few beasts that can survive in Skylands' snowy realms, but the Chillydogs love chilling out here. These playful ice-hounds keep warm with a thick layer of fur and the occasional snowball fight.

LEVIATHAN

The Leviathan are fearsome fish. They're not at all fussy about what goes into their mouths (which are crammed full of 1,672 super-sharp teeth!). Once, a Leviathan was so hungry it devoured a whole village!

Waterland

TURTLES

Turtles are totally laid-back creatures and never, ever rush anywhere (some might even call them lazy). Chances are they will get in your Skylander's way and slow them down to their own excruciatingly slow pace.

GOBBLE PODS

These plant-like creatures are always hungry. They hardly ever close their mouths in the hope of getting something yummy to eat! They look vicious but Skylanders shouldn't worry—Gobble Pods prefer to scoff Greebles.

WHY IS KAOS so EVIL?

Everyone knows Kaos is horrible but no one is quite sure how this former prince ended up as the most evil Portal Master in Skylands. Surely there must be a reason Kaos is so desperate for world domination? Was it his early life experiences that made him so mean, or was he simply born with an evil streak?

HIS UPBRINGING

Evil runs in Kaos's family. Kaos's Mom was a terrible influence when he was growing up as she always encouraged him to do evil. Now Kaos wants to prove to her just how horrible he has become.

HIS FRIENDS

Kaos's loyal sidekick Glumshanks is the closest thing he has to a friend, but the dutiful Troll never questions the actions of his bitter and twisted boss. Maybe if Glumshanks told Kaos that all his plans were terrible, Kaos might be less villainous!

HIS SKYLANDER OBSESSION

Every time Kaos is defeated by the Skylanders it makes him more determined to succeed. The mad mogul has become obsessed with beating the Skylanders, driving him to devise ever more desperate schemes. As his plans grow more dastardly, Kaos only becomes more evil.

HIS NATURE

Are Kaos's Mom, Glumshanks, and the Skylanders really to blame for his evil nature? These things may have helped Kaos grow into a truly gruesome grown-up, but perhaps he was simply evil from day one. Kaos has certainly never tried to be good. It's always possible that he is just plain mean.

IF YOU REALLY TRY, GLUMSHANKS, ONE DAY YOU COULD BE AS MEAN AS ME!

THE LIFE CYCLE OF A CHOMPY

Chompies are small green creatures with large teeth and little brains. They are a common sight in Skylands, but their natural tendency to bite means most inhabitants of Skylands find them a bit of a pain. These misunderstood monsters do have one fan—a wizard known as the Chompy Mage. He knows that when Chompies bark and bite, they are simply trying to say hello!

THE CHOMPY CYCLE

The Skylanders find Chompies' constant biting so annoying that they despatch them on sight. These nasty nibblers might not live long, but they certainly make the most of their time in Skylands.

1. A POD EMERGES
The life cycle of a Chompy begins in a large plant called a Chompy Pod. These pods provide a safe nest for developing Chompies and are found all over Skylands.

6. DESTROYED
When these pests cross paths with a busy Skylander, a Chompy often gets squashed. However, new Chompy pods are spawned all the time, so Skylands is always full of annoying new Chompies.

CHOMPY MAGE

The Chompy Mage is so obsessed with Chompies that the highlight of his year is the annual convention for Chompies, ChompyCon. This weird and wacky wizard even dresses like a Chompy, in a Chompy-style hood, and has a homemade Chompy glove puppet.

CHOMPING TEETH

EYE STALK

GIANT CHOMPY
The Chompy Mage likes to use his magical powers to transform into a colossal Chompy. The giant critter has the ability to release Chompy Eggs that hatch into Chompies.

LEAVES

2. BIRTH

The plant opens up to release fully grown Chompies. Each Chompy shoots out of the plant and takes its very first steps in Skylands.

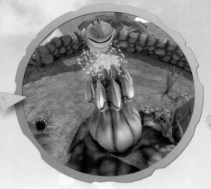

Did you know?

The Chompy Mage really likes Chompies, but he has other loves, too. He enjoys singing karaoke and eating enchiladas. Though not as much as he likes Chompies.

3. CHOMPY EGGS

Chompies are also created when the Giant Chompy lays his Chompy Eggs. Each Chompy Egg hatches a single Chompy.

4. A CHOMPY FLOCK

Chompies are always found with other Chompies. They love to make new friends, but other creatures prefer to avoid their toothy grins.

5. ATTACK!

A Chompy's natural instinct is to bite, and they like to get their large teeth stuck into almost anything. This often gets them into trouble.

OTHER CHOMPIES

These creatures might not look exactly like their green cousins, but they are all chomping Chompies. These Chompy varieties have adapted to be even better at biting and to cause even more chaos.

BONE CHOMPY
This bony creature has extra strong teeth.

CHOMPY FROSTFLOWER
These icy Chompies are far cooler than other Chompies.

ARMORED CHOMPY
Armored Chompies are protected by their helmets.

CHOMPY BOT 9000
Red Chompies pilot these Chompy-firing machines.

SKYLANDS' MOST WANTED

Have you seen these frightening fiends? Do you recognize these rotten rogues? These vile villains are all very good at being very bad, and their evil actions have put the innocent inhabitants of Skylands at risk. It is up to the Skylanders to find their hiding places and defeat them. If you spot any of them around Skylands, approach them with extreme caution!

IT IS UNWISE TO UNDERESTIMATE THESE ENEMIES, PORTAL MASTER.

CLUCK

THREAT LEVEL **5**

This plucky bird grew tired of the constant bellringing in his home of Clocktown, so he donned a giant mechanical suit that enabled him to stop time from flowing properly. It's up to the Skylanders to stop Cluck from trapping all of Skylands in an infinite time loop!

EVILIZED KAOS

THREAT LEVEL **10**

This is our old enemy Kaos, only taller, stronger, and uglier, with bigger fists and bigger feet! Some Petrified Darkness crystals fell on top of the pesky Portal Master and turned him into Evilized Kaos. Now, when Kaos has a tantrum, his huge feet cause serious shockwaves.

WARNING: THESE VILLAINS ARE DANGEROUS. ···· DO NOT APPROACH! ·

MESMERALDA

THREAT LEVEL **7.5**

Four-armed villain Mesmeralda is a truly twisted puppeteer who always puts on a grand show. She commands her dancing puppet chorus to project lethal wires across her stage. She also drops bombs to make her show (and Skylanders) go out with a bang!

SHEEP MAGE

THREAT LEVEL **5**

The Sheep Mage can turn anybody into a sheep with his magic staff. He can also change into a massive bleating monster-sheep that can suck victims towards him with one deep breath! The woolly wizard sees himself as avenging years of sheep mistreatment in Skylands.

FIRE VIPER

THREAT LEVEL **7.5**

The Fire Viper is an enormous snake-like monster. He loyally serves Kaos, breathing ferocious fire and coughing up big balls of lava at his enemies. The Fire Viper also has a particularly unpleasant personality—he loves to insult Skylanders.

KAOS'S MOM

Did you know?

Kaos's Mom uses the same method of communication as her son. They both like to talk through a giant floating image of their own heads. Subtle!

THREAT LEVEL **9**

If you thought Kaos was the biggest threat to Skylands, you obviously haven't met his mom! The self-proclaimed true dark Portal Master is over 100 years old, but age hasn't dimmed her dark desire for evil. She always plans her wicked schemes to perfection.

YOU SPOT ONE PLEASE CALL A SKYLANDER IMMEDIATELY!

GLOSSARY

AIRSHIP
A ship that can fly through the sky. Useful for getting around Skylands, if you don't mind the terrifying thought of flying.

ARKEYANS
An ancient race that ruled Skylands long ago. They specialized in building technological robots and machines.

ARKUS
The Arkeyans' major city. Also known as the Lost City of Arkus. Until it was found again. Then also known as the Found City of Arkus.

BENEVOLENT ANCIENTS
A mysterious race who lived before records began in Skylands. The Benevolent Ancients are believed to have built the Core of Light.

CHOMPY
An annoying pest commonly found in Skylands. Normally green and stupid, with lots of sharp teeth.

CITADEL
A strong fortress. A citadel used to stand alongside the Core of Light, but it was destroyed. Its remains can be found at The Ruins.

CORE OF LIGHT
An ancient machine that uses the eight known elements to produce a beam of light. This light counters the Darkness.

CYCLOPSES
Stinky creatures that are traditionally stonemasons. Now they generally work for Kaos, causing trouble.

THE DARKNESS
The force behind all evil in Skylands. Usually seen as dark, terrifying clouds.

DRAGON
A native Skylands species, which is strongly linked to the elements.

DROW
Elves who have been influenced by the Darkness and have turned evil. Kaos uses them as part of his army of minions.

EARTH
A bizarre world beyond Skylands. The Skylanders were teleported here after the destruction of the Core of Light. Master Eon trains new Portal Masters from Earth.

ELEMENT
Elements form the base of Skylands and everything in it. All eight known elements are equally powerful and create balance in Skylands.

ELEMENTAL GATE
An entrance to another world or area. Only Skylanders of the same element as the Gate can travel through it.

ENCHILADA
A delicious treat. Pure goodness, wrapped in a tasty tortilla, and topped with melted cheese. All creatures in Skylands love enchiladas.

ETERNAL SOURCE
The physical embodiment of each element used in the Core of Light. The Eternal Sources were scattered across Skylands when the Core was destroyed.

EVILIZE
To turn someone evil using Petrified Darkness crystals. A side effect of this is that the evilized creature often turns purple.

GIANTS
(Also known as Elder Elementals.) The original Skylanders who defeated the Arkeyans but were lost to Earth. They became legends in Skylands.

IRON FIST OF ARKUS
A huge, mechanical hand that belonged to the Arkeyan Kings. It has the power to create and control Arkeyan robots.

MABU
Some (Flynn) would say the Mabu are the greatest species in Skylands. Peace-loving, friendly, and helpful.

MINION
A general term for one of Kaos's lackeys. Minions are evil creatures who are always trying to stop the Skylanders from doing their job.

PETRIFIED DARKNESS
Purple crystals of solid Darkness. These gruesome gems have the power to turn creatures evil.

PORTAL
A magical gateway to another area of Skylands or another world.

PORTAL MASTER
A wise being who decides the fate of Skylands. Good Portal Masters recruit Skylanders to act as protectors against evil forces.

REALM
A general term for a land or island in Skylands.

ROBOTO BALL
An Arkeyan sport. It was considered exciting due to the tendency for roboto balls to explode during play.

SHEEP
Hugo believes these woolly creatures are pure evil. He thinks that they can't be trusted, that they steal, and that they are probably plotting to take over Skylands. They are actually harmless.

SKYLANDERS
An elite force of heroes dedicated to fighting evil and defending Skylands. Skylanders are linked to one of the eight known elements and have special powers.

SKYLANDS
A magical world consisting of countless floating islands in an endless sky.

SKYSTONES
A popular game in Skylands. Players try to win as many of their opponent's tiles as possible.

SWAP FORCE
A special team of Skylanders who have the power to swap their upper and lower bodies with each other, in order to merge powers.

TROLLS
Enemies of Skylanders who often work for Kaos. Some are skilled engineers, and most are mean.

THE UNDERWORLD
A shadowy, dark area of Skylands, full of ghosts and ghouls. Those who visit it risk becoming Undead themselves.

INDEX

Main entries are in **bold**

FAREWELL, YOUNG PORTAL MASTERS. UNTIL WE MEET AGAIN!

DK

LONDON, NEW YORK, MELBOURNE, MUNICH, and DELHI

Senior Editor Hannah Dolan
Designer Mark Richards
Editorial Assistant Beth Davies
Additional Designers Anne Staples and Elena Jarmoskaite
Additional Editors Jo Casey and Zoe Hedges
Pre-Production Producer Marc Staples
Senior Producer Alex Bell
Managing Editor Elizabeth Dowsett
Design Manager Ron Stobbart
Publishing Manager Julie Ferris
Art Director Lisa Lanzarini
Publishing Director Simon Beecroft

First published in the United States in 2014 by
DK Publishing
4th floor, 345 Hudson Street
New York, New York 10014

10 9 8 7 6 5 4 3 2 1
001–196548–July/14

A catalog record for this book is available from the Library of Congress.

ISBN: 978-1-4654-2129-6

Printed and bound in China by Leo Paper Products Ltd.
Color reproduction by Altaimage, UK

Picture credit (for the note paper on pages 18–19): Dreamstime.com: Mtkang.

**Discover more at
www.dk.com**